RAISING KIDS WHO ARE INFLUENCE PROOF

IRENE BANGWELL

Published in Nigeria by
Handz and Mindz Ltd
P.O. Box 8531,
Wuse, Abuja
Nigeria

First Edition
First Printing, 2019

ISBN: 9789-7897-2420-8

Cover Design
Vodina West
Lakitha Munasinghe

DEDICATION

To Briona & Elena Bangwell.
Kingsley & I are committed to supporting you
through every phase of life.

IRENE BANGWELL

BOOK MAP

ACKNOWLEDGMENTS

Taking up projects such as this requires having the right support system; spiritual support system, family support system, office team and friends who cheer you on.

I have been blessed with the gift of a strong support system and I have a lot to show for it. I took up a couple of writing projects at the same time including the writing of **Raising Kids Who Are Influence Proof** and my support system at every point in time, made it possible.

I also want to appreciate parents who have trusted me over the years with the mentoring of their children and teenagers. Thank you very much for the many learning opportunities you created for me. Thank you for your faith in me.

I would love to specially thank my fathers of faith for all I have learned from them and how these learnings have equipped and shaped me for what God wants of me. I would love to specially appreciate Pastor Andy & Ndidi Osakwe, Drs. Abel & Rachel Damina, Pastor Efezino & Folashade Idheze and Pastors Eshiet & Ofonime Udosen.

I would love to sincerely appreciate, my amazing husband, Kingsley Bangwell. There is no word to describe how blessed I am to have someone who sees what I can be and steadily reminds me to leave my mark in the world. I love you today and always.

I would also love to specially appreciate my brilliant daughters, Briona and Elena, who made the biggest sacrifice during the time of executing this book writing projects. For this, I appreciate them greatly.

Special thanks to my two foster daughters, Anurika Okoli and Rahab Kumbo, who stepped in, as they always do, to watch the girls and the home-front during these times. I pray that God blesses you greatly and raises help for you as you pursue greatness in your time.

To my amazing, brilliant, resourceful assistant, Sharon Ahumibe, I say, step out there, you have what it takes to live out the best version of your life. Thank you for being so prompt as you typed the manuscripts.

My profound gratitude goes to three amazing people who supported me through the writing of this book by reading through the manuscripts and taking the time to write the foreword as well as reviewing this book. They are Stella Nnodi, Wendy Ologe and Isang Awah. I appreciate you all greatly. Thank you so much for all your love.

Thank you, Valerie Vishnay & Mordecai Gbaratu, for being amazing and wonderful and patient too.

Thank you to great friends who lent professional help during these times especially Kaiso Dahnyels and Vodina West.

I would also like to say a very big thank you to my amazing mum, Odo Bassey Otu and my brother, Joshua Essien for their faith in me.

Everyone needs a tag team that believes in them completely and periodically calls them to order, so that one steadily defies the odds and lives out the very best version of their lives. Mine is made up of some of the most amazing people you can imagine. Thank you Mrs Angela Ajala, Mrs. Olusola Bankole, Emem Opashi, Tina Amachree, Kai Orga, Chidiebube Ocheme, Stephanie Itenebe, Wendy Ologe, Viviann Okoye, Rose Ojabo, Inimfon Etuk, Sam Obafemi, Aruk Eteng, Deborah Ikongbeh and so many other amazing people, thank you for your gift of beautiful friendship.

More than eleven years ago, I was so certain that I needed to write but there wasn't that much clarity of what I was going to write. For starters, I just could not get myself to eventually write. The projects I had started, as passionate as I was, I just couldn't bring myself to finish. Till date many of them remain unfinished.

Then Grace happened! Taking me totally on a different journey and pathway than I could ever have thought or imagine. Unprecedented.

Four published works, two manuscripts and two outlines later, I have come to return all the glory and honor to the King. Yes, to the maker of times, seasons, graces and places. The one who created me for His own good pleasure, glory and purpose.

Every single thought, insight, knowledge, you would find in these pages are God-breathed. He created all of the events from which I came to draw insights and meaning from.

The strongest memory I have throughout these writing projects is putting pen to paper and just finding words pour out in dimensions I have never thought about. At the weirdest of places and in very awkward moments, I have felt the urge to write and then it just poured out.

I have experienced a divine phenomenon.

This is the Father's time for these learnings. It's been a privilege being a part of this experience.

To the King of Kings and the Lord of Lords, I return ALL of the glory.

Irene Bangwell
Abuja, Nigeria
April 2019

FOREWORD

The purpose of this book can be summed up in these words, '...Essentially, we (parents and guardians) will ... raise ... children who ... will be independent, objective, stable and especially discerning ... and be able to help them understand or decode people from the place of their beliefs and motives so they can create healthy boundaries that helps them open up to the right kind of influence and shut out the wrong kinds of influence'.

Being the parent(s) of young children is not a walk in the park, let alone parenting teenagers. It isn't at all! As adolescents, their hormones are raging, they are rearing to go (because they believe they are adults) and, as far as they are concerned, you the parent(s) is/are the villain.

In 1988, I was 14 and in JSS3; I honestly believed that my mother was not my real mum, because back then, she was constantly on my case, scolding, henpecking and finding fault with everything I did!

However, in hindsight, and with me being a mum to a teenager, I totally understand what my mum was doing: all her 'whining and bitching' was for my own good. She was, in her own way, trying to set me on the right path.

Constantly scolding me was how she knew to do what she knew!

Parenting, in this present dispensation, has changed and is still changing now, what with new ways of reprimanding, chastising and affirming our children and wards. With the advent, growth and proliferation of technology and lifestyle trends, the pressure on (our) children is humongous. We can only begin to imagine the magnitude of pressure they face every day in school and in the outside world generally.

The question now is: What do we, as parents, do about this? What can we do? How can we help them cope and overcome the shenanigans of life's vicissitudes? As our babies are badgered by the vagaries of life, HOW CAN WE HELP THEM?

This book in your hand is the answer!

I met Irene in 2013, both of us pregnant at that time. She had just moved with her family from Jos to Abuja and was brimming and foaming in the mouth with ideas and way-forward innovations on how to help teenagers and young people maximize their potentials. So far, she has not disappointed me, and she will not; you can take that to the bank!

Irene is constantly birthing systems and processes for young people. Her grit passion for children and youth is organic, real life and contagious. You cannot be in her presence, hear her talk about young people and not catch the fever. She is a virus; a good virus. Whenever I listen to her talk about the plans, she has for the education sector, for example, I marvel.

Her love and quest for excellence has led to her co-founding KNOSK, an education innovation company that focuses on actionizing learning, education research and providing parenting education.

Raising Kids Who Are Influence-Proof is one book that will answer the questions you have about relating with and raising your preteen and teenage child(ren). It will make your navigation through the maze that parenting is easy.

The nuggets shared in here are bulls-eye and tells that, as parents, through all that we do as custodians of young, budding and impressionable lives, the key thing in delivering on this parenting job is this: 'AAA' - Accept. Affirm. Authenticate.

Nnodi, Stella Uchechi
Author: Biographies Are A Joke
LinkedIn/Instagram/Twitter/FB: dGrammarQueen

THE THING ABOUT WORKING TITLES
(INTRODUCTION)

Pressure. Peer pressure.

What does it mean for a child to be under peer pressure?

It means the child has a need to do the same things as other people of his or her age and social group in order to be liked or respected by them.

The pop-up words here are "need to be liked" or "respected by them".

As I began working on this book, several thoughts began playing in my head. The first would be interacting with the subject of influence.

Influence has been defined by Oxford dictionary as the capacity to have an effect on the CHARACTER, development or behavior of someone or something.

Merriam Webster considers influence as being indirect, or intangible. Meaning that it can be subtle. It can go unnoticed. It also refers to it as a corrupt interference with authority for personal gain.

Dictionary.com refers to influence as the capacity or power of a person or things to be a compelling force that produce effects on the actions, behavior, opinions of others.

Collins Dictionary takes it further by defining it as the power to make other people agree with your opinions or do what you want.

There are several words coming out of these perspectives to what influence is.

The first involves changing the course or direction in which a person or thing was going or where it had the tendency to go.

That is why influence is expressed through words like 'DERAIL' and 'SWAY.

Influence affects character development and behavior. In the definition by dictionary.com, we see it in the way influence is represented as a force that produces effects on the actions (what a person does) at a given time, behavior (the way a person acts towards others and in different situations) and opinions (what a person thinks about certain things) of others.

Based on all of the above definitions, my definition of influence would be a conscious or unconscious introduction of new ideas that shape what a person does, how a person acts towards others and in response to different situations as well as what a person believes is right or wrong.

The goal of influence is usually for cohesion. People seek to influence others so that they all can think alike and this usually gives a sense of togetherness.

While I started out on my thoughts on this, I asked myself, is influence always a bad thing?

Definitely not!

Looking at all the definitions and references we have drawn thus far, you find that if a person was going in the wrong direction, the right kind of influence can move them in right direction.

In the same breath, if a person was moving in the wrong direction still, the wrong kind of influence can push them even further along on the wrong path.

Influence can move a person out of a right or wrong path or it can push them further along on whatever paths they were already on; right or wrong.

This book is therefore designed to help us parents achieve three things:
   a. Show/teach/inspire our children to stay focused on the right path in-spite of what they may be up against.
   b. To help our children identify the right kind of influence when it comes.
   c. To help our children identify the wrong kind of influence when it comes.

Essentially, we will not raise naive children who do not know which is which; they will be independent, objective, stable and especially discerning.

Parents application of what is learned in this book will

help our teens understand or decode people from the place of their beliefs and motives so they can create healthy boundaries that helps them open up to the right kind of influence and shut out the wrong kinds of influence.

When I chose this title, I had to deal with the internal debate of whether or not 'influence-proof' was a fair enough word to use in the context of influence being good or evil. Then I realized that putting the control back in the hands of a child to choose whether or not they want to yield to any kind of influence especially the right kind, means they have control.

Thereby, making this title suitable for my message.

Think about this book as a resource on balancing out.

- **Key Points**

- Influence is a conscious introduction of ideas that shape how we think, what we do and how we do certain things.
- Influence can encourage a child to stay on the right path: in which case it is considered positive or the right kind of influence.
- Influence can also move a child out of the right path into the wrong path.
- Influence can motivate a child who was already on the wrong path to continue even further on the wrong path.

WHERE DOES INFLUENCE COME FROM?
(CHAPTER ONE)

Where does influence come from?

Recall my definition of influence from the previous chapter as 'a conscious or unconscious introduction of new ideas that shape what a person does, how a person acts towards others and in response to different situations as well as what a person believes is right or wrong'.

Knowing what the sources of influences are, can be an amazing self-protection and self-preservation tool. In this chapter, using a personal story, I get to show us some of the places where influence begins.

In this chapter, I literally pull out where and how these new ideas are introduced. Even as adults, we get caught in this web. I recommend that you read this chapter as though you were the one who needed to rise above influence. It will empower you to know where and how to take charge.

I recall a time in my teen years when I misfired seriously, fashion-wise. I grew up in the serene city of Calabar in Nigeria. I am not so certain if Calabar fits into the true definition of a small town but it is widely believed that everyone knew everyone. You were either classmates in primary or secondary school, or went to the same church or were neighbors with someone who was a cousin or relative to someone in school etc.

It was a mid-term holiday in 1996 and I had gone visiting a great grand uncle, who was the patriarch of our extended family. His home was the meeting point for all of our relatives; the rich and everyone else. His home was always a beehive of activities.

I had cousins who came in from Lagos and other cities, who probably went to much better schools than I did and, quite frankly, seemed to be a lot more exposed. They had book, laptops, really nice clothes and were the real definition of awesome.

That mid-term holiday, I was almost certain they were going to be home and I just had to look my best. I mean, you know, I just had to, or so I thought.

So, feeling very proud of myself, I wore the Efik traditional attire called 'Onyonyo'.

Onyonyo is your typical Elizabethan dress pattern only that it's made with Ankara (African fabric) which makes it more beautiful in my Nigerian opinion.

So on this memorable day, I wore this with a pair of sneakers. Yep! You read right. Whaaat?! Who does that? Onyonyo on sneakers?!

Well, in a bid to impress, I did.

While I have no memory of my cousins' response or reactions I do recall resuming school the very next week only to find that a classmate had seen me on my way and brought the gist to school.

At the time in school, whenever we ran into a school mate, the gist had a way of always coming up at school. So if you told a school mate that you saw another school mate during the holidays, the first thing they would ask would be "what did she wear?".

So, someone saw me and mentioned that I wore 'Onyonyo and sneakers' and everyone was talking about it. I denied it outrightly while quietly hoping to find out who said it.

I was so embarrassed. For the next few weeks, I was miserable. Today, I am thankful it didn't happen in 2019. If it did, the impact would have been much worse.

For one, the person would be bolder to approach me and take a picture or take one from wherever; which would have been an attack the moment it happened. That would, as a result, completely ruin my day and get me anxious about resuming school. The said picture would have been shared online, starting with platforms such as WhatsApp. Who knows, maybe a classmate would create a meme or two and I would have gotten really crazy comments from people who didn't know me and may have gone beyond what I wore to talk about other body parts.

Bottom line: It was the perfect case for today's online shaming culture

From this story, I would like to pull out the thread of influence in yesterday's teen culture and today's teen reality.

By the thread of influence, I want to show how belief

defines opinions, choices, actions, expectations and, ultimately, how influence thrives.

1. Exaggerated interpretations.

Example; "EVERYONE KNOWS EVERYONE".

It's a small world, but everyone does not know everyone. It's amazing how much lies and deception is out there on the basis of the simple word "EVERYONE".

Many of our children have been coerced to do things from the place of fear that 'EVERYONE' does this or that or will do this or that. Sometimes that is fear is more present than reality and will be a source of big influence.

The simple belief that everyone knows everyone, in itself, creates room for fear-based decision making.

2. Exaggerated attribution of importance.

Influence thrives on what anyone considers as important. In my case in the story, I made the opinion of my classmates too much important. Infact, overly important. What I may not have realized today was people forget, people define things from their own points of view, people are carried away by pressing issues, people are busy and so on and so forth. If all the girls in my school heard about it, which I really doubt, they would not have thought the exact same thoughts. A few of them may probably have worn the exact same combination. Perhaps, if I had just turned around and made a joke of it, I wouldn't have been so embarrassed and ashamed.

Many teens today and understandably so, place the ideas of what their mates think over what their parents think or expect because they have not been taught from early enough that the views of people may not be as important as we make it.

3. My cousins were not superior.

I didn't need to try to impress anyone. The consideration of one person as superior over the others is subjective. Meaning that it is only as real as you believe it.

In very many ways it comes from our own insecurity. We must know that regardless of our differences, we all bring something to the table. When we meet people, we should offer what we have that will serve the relationship. We cannot afford to compare ourselves through the course of our life. That would be a waste of our precious potentials.

In the course of our children transiting from pre-puberty to puberty years, you would notice the need to compare and the subjective conclusions they will easily make. As parents, we must be there to tell and remind them that many times, what they think in their heads is not always the reality.

4. Blinded perspectives.

Put differently, each fashion item was beautiful. The dress was gorgeous and so were the sneakers. They were just not to be worn together in those times. There were also girls at school who may not have had the Onyonyo itself and those who may not have had a pair of sneakers either. So, there were those who would have thought I was a big fish.

Influence always tries to blind us to full reasoning of the subject matter from different points of view. Many children and teenagers who are badly influenced, do not see the whole picture.

5. Complex plus the need for validation.

There is the 'fear of shame' and there is also the 'need for validation' which usually plays out as the need to be seen as a force to be reckoned with. Some children and teens want to be the loved ones, the celebrated ones, the popular ones. This need makes them desperate enough to call out or ridicules others. Think about the classmate who brought my Onyonyo gist to school. What do you think she was trying to achieve?

The driving thought or belief is to sound to peers that one has superior judgment. Funny enough, people do this for the sole reason of winning friends and gaining validation, without much consideration for the person whose reputation they deride in the cause of building theirs.

We should be teaching our children that empathy should be at the foundation of the choices they make. At KNOSK, we believe that empathy is one of the pillars of influence-proof living.

Just taking the time to think about how their own choices will affect the next person, their teachers and classmates can help them keep their heads over the waters of cold insensitivity to others.

Parents need to from cradle model empathy, by steadily having conversations and making considerations about how their own actions as parents may affect their children and how the children's individual actions may affect their siblings and even other people outside of the family.

This can tame insecurity especially at the level where it regulates the kinds of actions a child will take as a result of insecurity.

6. Categorisation.

Many times, influence is that voice that makes you uncomfortable around someone. When you think that a person is superior to you, you place a demand on yourself to act a certain way. This is influence as it strives to shape your reaction towards others.

We create compartments and definitions of what people are and define or create rules about who we should be when around certain people.

From all of these, we see that first influence can begin from an external situation but for it to take effect, there has to be an internal acceptance.

I had to have accepted that everyone at school had heard about what I wore.

I had to have accepted the opinions of my peers as law.

I had to have accepted that I needed to impress my cousins.

Young people have to accept that they are not good enough and so shaming others makes them feel powerful and strong.

I have to accept that a person is a certain way for me to act in a certain way while I am with them.

All of these narratives listed from #1 to #6, and even more that you may have spotted on your own or from your own life's experiences make up how influence comes.

So, influence is the most convincing when it is subtle. It is like an idea that has been meditated on.

To effectively deflect the impact of these wrong influences, we must address the basics of what our children believe about themselves and the meanings they make out from all that is happening around them.

?

So where are the places our children pick up perspectives that become an influence?

At Home

Yes, this is the very first place children pick up influence and sometimes the home can be the source of the wrong kind of influence.

Excessively categorizing rich and poor has an impact on what your child believes, expects, demands and responds to.

Exaggerations beget exaggerations, whether it be of value or numbers. As parents, we should speak in plain terms with our children.

For instance, it is safer to say three people called to ask blah blah blah instead of saying 'everyone was calling.' Always take note of 'everyone' stories.

Comparing our children or hailing one over the other sets them up for a pursuit of validation of which, when the habit begins, there are no boundaries.

They will seek validation from teachers and young people of the same or opposite sex and sometimes even with complete strangers. Once a child seeks to impress without a healthy motive or background, it can be a pretty desperate place.

Our children will try to make us happy. They should. But it should not be because they want to outdo each other. The goal is to see them do it together or remind each other to do it and that will essentially balance out.

Home is the most interesting place for influence. Relatives live with us and pour their own bits of influence into our children - good or bad.

Where else does influence come from?

School

This is the place where children with different influences from their homes come and try to suppress, without necessarily intending to, all that parents have been teaching. To make it even more interesting, the children with our own children at school, probably spend longer hours with our children. Perhaps longer that we do.

At school, certain children also come with their opinions and strive to shove it on others. They create parameters and expect a lot of other children to buy into such because for what they are trying to achieve, numbers can be the defining factor.

In many cases, they are louder and more forceful than the average child. They may even bully others into believing what they believe and make those children act the way they want them to.

Pop-culture

This is short for 'popular culture'. It refers to generally recognized practices, beliefs and objects that are dominant or ubiquitous in a society <u>at a given point in time.</u>

So, pop-culture is essentially what is believed to be cool, true, or brilliant in each generation or at different points in time.

Pop-culture cuts across fashion, language, behavior codes, ideologies, etc. and they are mostly propagated through entertainment as seen in literature, fashion, arts, music, dance, celebrity culture and cyber culture.

Popular culture is very pervasive. Our young ones see it in their peers, on TV, hear it as lyrics in music, and on the internet, which also allows them close in on the lifestyles of celebrities who, up and close on social media, express various aspects of pop-culture.

Through pop-culture, young people are influenced by new belief systems such as what to do to get respect and popularity, why you need respect and popularity, whether to do drugs, have a tattoo, or get a piercing or perhaps what pyjamas to wear when taking a night time selfie for instance.

Young people pick cross cutting themes of what the priority for their lives should be and then go out there (school, home etc.) to live out what pop-culture suggests.

Today's teens are perhaps more bombarded than we ever were. There is 24-hour access to TV shows. There's also the ever alert social media that pushes pop-culture through direct entertainment and people's attempt at interpreting pop-culture themselves which makes it an everyday, all round the clock, subtle and extremely effective source of influence.

Popular culture is so effective that corporations follow

it in creating advertising and designing products for certain age groups.

What makes it crazy is when pop-culture okays risky behavior.

The #MeToo movement revealed the role pop-culture played on a generation. There was a time that it was cool to drug girls and rape them at a party.

There was a time pop-culture was okay with gang-raping and because pop-culture, at that time, said it was okay, young men drew validation from doing so and publicly boasting about it thereby fueling very disturbing behavior.

Unfortunately, pop-culture doesn't necessarily ever throw up stronger values. Hardly does it. You watch movies and see the continual tendency to less and less clothing, nudity, the creation and definition of words like 'sexy' and their meanings and after one sees a movie, unconsciously, they tend towards what the movies portray. For example, they may begin to speak like the characters in the movie and more often than not, people also adopt the mind-set and values captured in the movies, into their lives in reality.

Pop-culture has two things we have to always probe into: the brains behind the original idea of these concepts and the fuel for it.

We need to ask, who started this culture. Why is it appealing to young people?

For example, you notice a new culture of say sagging trousers. It will be more helpful as a parent, to find out where it all started as well as why it appeals to young people before you start criticizing and telling them to stop.

With the billions of people all over the world, regardless of race, tribe or nationality, enjoying unrestricted access to a single platform such as Facebook, anybody, whether sick, poorly informed or just in a really foul mood, can come online and start just about anything.

For some, it's a social media challenge, others with skills create games that push whatever values they are passionate about and for others, they have talents and the resources to push their imaginations which sometimes is sick. You see movies that are purely fictions of a director's imagination. Asking who is behind a particular pop-culture practice can help us deflate its potency.

Infact, someone can create an online game that tends towards pornography for our children and teens. We should ask our children to find out who built or owns the game platform. The search should be with the goal of understanding where the originator is coming from. What do they believe? What do they represent?

The process of asking these questions, essentially demystifies the image that the trend is trying to create around the subject.

Efforts such as this is geared towards using logic and objectivity to swallow up what is generally popular.

Popularity usually means that a new idea or trend is acceptable.

Why are these strange ideas usually acceptable by young people?

Pop-culture thrives on CONTROVERSY. What people generally believe cannot be done, pop-culture does and, in the process, reduces the meter/measurement for morality. And this always gets the audience in awe - an extreme emotional state that tends towards admiration of the courage that it took to pull it through.

A young man for instance, begins to go online to show himself in pictures and videos as a cross dresser. This is the real definition of controversial. He has stepped outside of what young boys will easily do. So, by the time this online 'super star' begins to wear make-up, fix weavons just like women, his courage draws extreme admiration and extreme disgust. Either ways they will draw attention.

One of the other things that allows pop-culture thrive amongst young people is the 'need' to belong. The human need for intimate relationship and friends comes naturally to every one of us.

Pop-culture serves as a common thread that runs through the lives of children and teens giving them a common experience, shared allegiances and a place of identity and belonging.

The fashion approach of each generation gives everyone in that generation a sense of belonging. There was the afro generation, the hipsters and pedal pushers' generation, the oleku generation and today the weaves generation. All of the afore-mentioned have all been fashion trends in Nigeria.

Are you even a part of your generation if you do not wear what the trends are?

It will interest you to know that 'pop-culture' is first and foremost experienced by our children through cartoons.

Recently, I heard my two daughters speak freely about concepts that were completely alien to us: "hypnotize" and "yoga" drawn from a cartoon show they watched. I have seen them try to change the way they walk, express excitement, gesticulate all as a result of cartoons. Pop-culture as a source of influence and peer-pressure is extremely fluid.

Influence ('a conscious or unconscious introduction of new ideas that shape what a person does, how a person acts towards others and in response to different situations as well as what a person believes is right or wrong') is taking place at home, at school and everywhere around us and our children. This pollination thrives in the subtlety of its approaches. It is happening so quietly that it can easily be missed.

How can you raise a child today who is not adamant to this on-going, steady, and consistent surge to pollinate their mindsets, beliefs etc., even when it meets their need to belong?

-   Key Points

- Influence begins with the little things that we believe. Things like what is important and what is not., who is important and who is not.

- Not thinking through the things, we believe will make influence overwhelm us.

- Influence on children begins at home. What we say as parents, what other people in our homes say, what our children are exposed to become ideas they have that eventually become influence.

- Children are also influenced at school by other children bringing what they have learned from their own families.

WHAT DOES INFLUENCE LOOK LIKE?
(CHAPTER TWO)

Here, I take us on a journey to what peer pressure looking like for children of different ages. The goal is to show us how from cradle, we can set off to raise children who are not easily influenced by what is happening around them.

Most people are familiar with 'peer pressure'. While growing up, a number of Non-governmental Organizations (NGOs) and adults were talking about it. Reading from the beginning, one would very easily know that the word 'influence' could very easily pass for peer pressure and, for sure, it will in nearly every context, especially after we have established that influence can be positive or negative. Likewise, peer pressure can be positive or negative.

There are certain needs that are inherent to human beings. Yes, all of us. Which is why the first thing to take into consideration is that your child is not immune to peer pressure.

There are inherent needs that make teens, for example, prone to peer pressure, and knowing what these needs are can be a strategic first step to helping your child soar above the tide.

These needs include;

1. The fear of not having friends to hang out with;
2. The fear of being rejected or criticized;

3. The fear of embarrassment or judgment;
4. The need to boost their esteem and popularity;
5. The need to experiment and figure out who they are; and
6. The need to belong and the sense of safety that it brings.

Adolescents particularly develop a strong desire to fit in with their peers and be accepted, thus making peer pressure tough to resist. Interestingly, peer pressure exists for all ages and begins early on in life, when children have the cognitive capacity to compare themselves with others.

In toddlers, as soon as they are up to the age of two, they can want things just because other children have same. This can affect a child's behavior and other aspects of their life.

In pre-school, a child can go out of their way to do something they have seen a peer repeatedly do even though they know it outrightly contradicts what they have been taught by their parents.

It doesn't take long before they begin to make demands for things they didn't usually demand for.

Research shows that between ages five to eight, children are proactive towards pleasing their friends and peers. If the friends have positive values, this can be a plus but how about when it's negative?

The pre-teen and teen years happen to be the years where peer-pressure is strongest. As they grow into adolescents, they become increasingly concerned about belonging to a group with their peers. During this time, puberty sets in and they begin to feel like they have "come of age" and as such they underestimate their need for parental guidance.

During these times, peer relationships become their source of advice, socializing and entertaining activities.

Signs of Peer Pressure

1. Girls shortening their skirts or trying to use heavy makeup.
2. Boys experimenting with smoking, drinking alcohol or other illegal activities.
3. When they stop hanging out with friends or peers you (parents) approve of.
4. When they are overly obsessed with missing out or not fitting in.
5. When they develop a negative attitude.
6. When they begin to lie, cheat or be deceitful.
7. Changing the way they talk.
8. Choosing the same clothes, hairstyle or jewelry as a friend or celebrity.
9. Making their hair a certain way.

What Can A Teen Be Pressured To Do?

A teen can be pressured to:

1. Use alcohol, drugs, cigarettes etc.
2. Date, have sex, watch porn or sexting etc.
3. Bully others online and offline.
4. Pressure to diet or body build.
5. Disregard school work- skip classes, turn in assignments late, cheat on a test.
6. Stealing.

Let me punctuate here that there are group effects to peer pressure. In many cases, teens within a group can all be pressured by pop-culture trends and they are essentially all responding to it, how they know best. So there may be no name and face behind the activities leading them.   Pop-culture places a demand.

Many times, parents are quick to want to point out the one child who is 'spoiling' their own children. You would be surprised to know hat there are real cases where all of them are equally pressured and they are all responding the best way they know how to.

Sometimes peer pressure can be direct where there is someone telling them what to do. Sometimes, this someone can be a Youtuber and a person they hold in high esteem.

It can be indirect where a group of friends do something together but each one is not likely to do it on their own or when they are alone.

Peer pressure can be spoken. Here, a request is made directly to the child requiring him to take an action or discouraging him or her from taking an action.

Through spoken or verbal pressure a teen can be asked to do something and shamed publicly when he or she refuses to.

Unspoken peer pressure involves using gestures. A look of approval or disapproval by one person or group of people at another. It can involve smirks, shrugs, shoves and in Nigerian parlance basically body language.

What makes peer pressure thrive?

1. Having fewer boundaries from home. Parents who are too permissive and indulgent model openness to low standards for the children thus making them far more susceptible to peer pressure than those with firm expectations.
2. Too busy parents who are not proactively involved in their children's lives have not sufficiently built them up to be able to stand up for themselves.
3. Teens are inundated with what other people think of them which in turn decreases their self-esteem. They care far too much about the opinions of others. Sometimes, they say they don't, but this is not true as they actually do very much. And when you hear a teen saying 'they do not care what people think', very often, they are most likely referring to the peers who are unpopular or the adults who are trying to keep them on track.
4. The teen's prefrontal cortex, the part of the brain which helps moderate emotional and impulse control, is not fully developed until the early mid-twenties.
5. During the teen years, teens are more interested in their peers' opinions than those of their parents or adults. This is different for teens who have a healthy relationship from the get go with their parents.

Peer Pressure and Mental Health

Teens are under constant pressure - pressure from pop-culture, pressure to excel academically, pressure to become their own person independent of their parents and guardians while also dealing with the hormonal and physical changes their body is undergoing.

When it comes to peers, they are dealing with the constant pressure to fit in and to gain approval which can eventually become overwhelming and result in depression and other health issues.

You see, for teenagers, the pressure to conform and be approved by peers is desperate. School is full of cliques.

There is often times pressure to pretend that they are someone they are not. This complicates their struggle to find who they are in this mix where they are even pretending and masking the bits, they already know about themselves.

The discomfort induced by the confusion can cause teens to suffer from low self-esteem, anxiety and depression. Typically, one day, they are trying to find out if blue is really their favorite color and the very next day someone is saying that people who love blue are gloomy and boring.

This can be very confusing and overwhelming.

Signs Your Child is Suffering from Depression

1. Constant sadness, irritability and lack of energy.
2. Low moods, tearfulness or feelings of hopelessness.
3. Sudden change in behavior
4. Reluctance to go to school.
5. Withdrawal from activities they used to enjoy.
6. Loss of appetite or overeating.
7. Sudden drop in academic performance
8. Constant complaints of being bored or unengaged.
9. Self imposed isolation.
10. Sudden weight loss or weight gain.

- Key Points

- Peer pressure begins in children from the time they are toddlers.
- Peer pressure can lead to serious mental health challenges such as depression, which can affect a child's life in entirety including school work.
- In teenage years, peer pressure is the strongest because of the strong pull to fit in with peers.
- Peer pressure is one of the reasons for teens engaging in risky behaviours.
- When parents are too busy to spend time with their children, they create a void. This void can be not investing enough time in building a child's self esteem or teaching them how to handle peer pressure.

WHAT SHOULD YOU DO AS A PARENT?
(CHAPTER THREE)

Whether you are seeing signs of full blown influence or you are just concerned that your child may be gullible, or maybe you just want to prepare your child ahead, in this chapter, I lay out steps to take that would help you build a strong base of support for your child.

1. Keep an open, honest and close relationship with your children. By this I mean, strive to be the go-to person for your children.

This should not happen when they are teens but right from their childhood. Walking into their room when they are teens and saying "I am your friend; you can talk to me" sounds a bit weird and awkward especially when you have steadily worn the parent cap.

Sometimes, we like to think that parenting is effective when we are instructive and forceful. I have learned that parenting must involve setting standards and children can be inspired to take the right steps other than always getting into coercive interaction.

If there is a relationship, then instructions will be followed willingly and not forcefully.

So how do we cultivate this?

<u>Be an active listener.</u>

Listen over the years. Listen from when they are toddlers, to when they are preschoolers, to when they are of school age, to pre-teen years and it will naturally lead to conversations during teen years. Listen for their excitement, beliefs, misconceptions etc.

<u>Keep communication free of judgment and labelling.</u>

You could say I don't judge or label my children, if in the cause of conversations, you label others then you set precedence that makes your children believe that you are coming for them next.

For many parents, it is the reverse. You judge their every action and this scares them for staying in relationship with you.

You have to stick with principles BUT you have to be judgment free and open to having conversations with them.

<u>Don't, from childhood, wait for your child to ask for a time to talk to you. Create the opportunity for a conversation.</u>

Call your children and periodically chat about anything. Let the children see that they can talk about anything with you and you are genuinely interested in talking to them.

Create dates and opportunities to talk as a group, howbeit, make the time to talk to one child at a time too.

During cluster conversations, have everyone share highs and lows of their day. Cultures such as this should be encouraged from the time children are really young.

I recall the moment I started speaking individually with my second. I think she was between three or four years old. I told her I wanted us to have a conversation and it just literally blew her away.

Ever since that day and especially at the onset it is not unusual to hear her say, "mummy, can we have a conversation?"

<u>Be respectful in all forms of communication.</u>

Create an atmosphere at home that is warm. Whether it's communication to change the TV channel, or to pick up their shoes or even litter, keep the communication firm yet respectful. Name calling should not be allowed from both children and parents. All of these helps you keep an open, honest and close relationship with your children.

Other things to do to help your child include;

2. Resist school cultures that lead to peer pressure.
Different schools are proactive about creating fun experiences for children but sometimes do not realize that some cultures fuel peer pressure. One thing that happens all the time at schools is children celebrating their birthdays. Teachers need to de-emphasize how each child celebrates.

Some teachers knowingly or unknowingly set parents up to outdo themselves thus setting precedence for peer pressure. A teacher will say for example, for Uti's birthday, we want this and that, so that it will be beautiful.

As a parent, I have learnt to smile and do what I want, how I want and when I want without the pressure to impress anyone. If I as a parent, get pressured to do, I model to my child to give in to peer pressure.

If possible, break the tide, create your own family tradition for marking birthdays. Create your family's tradition for graduation. Let the children see that we are not competing but celebrating.

However, create traditions that your children are connected to. Something that is so fun for them that the norm falls like a house of cards.

So last year after my second child's birthday in September, I mentioned to my daughters that we will no longer do birthday goodie-bags or party packs. I went further to say, "it's your birthday it should be all about you".

What would you like to do for fun? One said she would like to swim and the other said she would like to have some ice-cream. I then said, "sure you will take a cake to class but after school it's going to be about 'YOU'".

3. Always ask for "what they really want." Peer pressure is actually about groups coercing each other to go along with certain beliefs or behaviors and in many cases harshly disapproving of those who do contrary.

What this means is that in many cases, teens under peer pressure know what they want. It could be buried under a lot of pretense and 'cock and bull' stories. As a parent with a great relationship with your child, you have to ask them, at all times, what they really want.

Chances are, they do not like what they are doing but don't have the courage to think it through and act on what they really want.

 If your child is happy with who they are, their choices and values, they are less likely to be influenced by other people.

4. Let your teens see the world. The teenage years are characterized by narrow-mindedness and short-sightedness. As parents, our core responsibility is to expose our teens to other perspectives.

From childhood, expose them to concepts such as two different sides to a story, the multiple endings of one story and this we can literally facilitate by exposing our teens to reading, arts, creative activities with individual and group dynamics.

Let us make learning immersive by opening casual conversations on the concepts, materials and anything else they are currently involved in.

Even in helping them resolve disputes, also help them see the other side of the story. In reading, ask them what if questions, which allow them to think outside of the box of any given reality per time.

All of these helps us maximize teachable moments.

5. Get to know their friends. Did you know that labelling your children's friends actually waters down your authority?

For starters, if you have once been a teen (which every parent has), then you would know that there were times our parents were wrong about the people who were negative influences on our lives.

Once a child shows up in your child's life, get to know the child, get to know the family they come from. Get to know their values without the mindset of finding how they may be a negative influence on your child.

You may be pleasantly surprised to find that they are not negative influences. At the same time, some of these children who show up as friends of our children who appear to be of the wrong kind of influence, are also going through peer pressure. They may be ahead of our children in experimenting but they are struggling and may need our help. You can and should create opportunities for conversations and nurturing.

6. Help amplify the voices of positive models. One of the indications of peer pressure is that many times, our children switch friends. When they do this, many things could be responsible. We, first and foremost, need to find out what it is.

Our teens are very quick to leave friends who seem to have values that go against what is trending or sometimes sound like their parents when they are at school. They may be perceived as boring.

We need to help those friends and encourage them to not allow our children topple over them. While you should not insist on the relationship, ensure that your child does not just shut the other child down.

The other child, in many cases, can be a sibling with a stronger voice of reason. Help them reach a place of appreciating and listening to each other.

7. Help your teen redefine friendship. During the teen years, teens are overly concerned about making and keeping friends. Helping them redefine who a friend is can start them out on a journey to resisting influence.

Help them see that:

"Same hairstyle, same gang, same fashion items" do not translate to the affection, sympathy and understanding that they need.

Some friends will abandon you when you are in need. Infact, Simon Sinek said in a recent research with millennials or so, that they agreed that their relationships were superficial. They knew that if they got into trouble, they could not count on their own friends to be there for them.

Let them also learn from your story of a failed friendship.

For teens, teach them the creed for defining friendship:

1. True friends speak truth.
2. True friends don't try to change you.
3. True friends listen to you and genuinely care for you.

4. True friends want to keep you out of trouble.
5. True friends talk about growth, improvement and commitment to study.
6. True friends do not want you in trouble with the authorities.

What else should make this list? Do well to add it.

<u>8. Parenting model matters</u>. In Africa, our parenting model is to steadily tell our children what to do. This doesn't allow our children and teens flex their decision-making muscles. Since they are so used to being told what to do, they tend to go off with every trend that pops up. This is because we always use the "do this", "say this" and all of those kinds of instruction models. These models shut off the development of the logical part of their brain. They just obey.

Unfortunately, there may very limited strength to resist the need to obey seeing that the muscle of logic has not been exercised.

Many times, we define our children's respect for us through these models but the truth is we are not in their lives to command obedience but frame character. The former involves obedience that may never include shaping of their character. But the latter includes them obeying - but obedience here will embody owning the values and beliefs that drive the obedience and shapes their character.

Simply put, the former involves obedience in front of you, the other is obedience whether you are there or not because they know why obeying is important.

As children and teens, we were raised to be obedient. That means take your parents' instructions without question, suggestions or recommendation.

Eventually as parents, that's how we flex our strong parent muscle but it is also the way we practice 'obedience without complaint'. Since our children's minds would have been trained to be obedient, it becomes their default response to instructions and suggestions.

We must break out of this mold. We must stop the "do it because I said so" tradition and allow for more and more dialogue, so that they can practice matching logic with recommendations.

What should you do instead, from a young age, to expose your children to decision-making dynamics and principles?

- Have them do chores.

- Have them plan for the next day of school.

- Expose them to the concept of personal responsibility as well as roles of service to others at home.

- Let them serve the guests. Let them ask the guests what they would like to have. Let them make decisions on alternatives to go for.

- When you instruct, allow them to ask questions.

- One aspect of strong peer influence is in what our teens wear. Have them pick out clothes and then approve and start this on early.

And don't approve or disapprove using your discretion. Use set parameters like:

- Is it clean?
- What's the temperature of the room we would be in?
- Do they usually use that outfit for any other activities?
- Is such an activity coming up soon?
- Do the colors go together?
- Is it decent?
- Does it feel comfortable to wear?
- Does it feel comfortable to walk in over long periods of time?
- What activity will they be involved in when they arrive a location? Will the attire be suitable for them to perform all those activities?

By the time we go over these kinds of questions, after a while, the children would learn new parameters beyond "it's trendy" for picking out clothes. But what I particularly love about this model is that it highlights how it should always be about what really works for them and not what someone somewhere who has no idea of their reality, is determining for them.

9. Create a culture that esteems and validates them holistically.

Accept. Affirm. Authenticate.

You have to accept your child. You may have had an idea of what your child should be like, you may have wanted him or her to be a certain way, behave, speak a certain way or perhaps you wish the gender was different. Welcome to what you have in your hands. Accept it so that you can see the beauty within.

There is no one model or prototype for what a successful child should be like. 'Best in science' is not the only parameter. Accept what you have as ENOUGH. Nurture your children in the best way possible and watch them shine.

Behind every child who believed in him or herself is a parent who believed in him/her first.

After accepting your child, you have to affirm this child consistently.

An affirmation is something we steadily say to and about a situation. Speaking long enough can have a significant impact on our mind's interaction with reality.

Hopefully, your affirmations are positive, because they can also be negative. If you repeatedly point out your child's inadequacies, that will have an impact on your mind and your child's mind's interaction with reality. You say it long enough, you come to believe it, you come to act like it and then you get a responsible response in reality.

This means that their minds will 'believe' a certain way and interpret events and situations in a particular manner.

For instance, if you steadily say that your child is stupid, even in situations where they are capable, they will believe they are incapable.

Seeing how incredibly powerful God has made the human brain, we have to proactively and deliberately feed the brain with what we want it to produce.

At KNOSK, we have broken down affirmation when it comes to parenting into three parts:

1. What we say in our heads about our children.
2. What we say to our children.
3. What we ask our child to say about him or herself.

From the time my first was three years old, I have made her say affirmations almost on a daily basis, at least five times a week. By the time the younger one was old enough, we got her saying those affirmations as well. Some of those words have formed the beliefs they have about themselves.

One year during the Christmas, I decided to buy two boxes of building blocks for my daughters. I must have missed that it was suitable for the older but not the younger in terms of the age specification. We found out when we got home.

For the first couple of days, she tried relentlessly to get building hers when she saw her elder sister doing hers. It was obvious that she was discouraged. One afternoon, I stepped out just in time to hear her older sister saying to her, 'you can do it. You know you can.'. I was really touched by this gesture.

A few days later, she helped her sister tweak a part of her own design and it was a milestone we all celebrated. Before the week was over, she had learnt how to build hers from scratch.

With our words, we enable or cripple them. So, say it in your head. Say it to them. Make them say it of themselves. Make them say it to each other.

Remember to show up and be a part of their lives. Show that you love them indeed.

The third part of this focuses on you becoming an "AUTHENTIC Parent". This begins with your 'why'.

Your children do not need to have an A because you had an A. They should because they are capable of it and we must also work to support them if they fall short. It should not be a problem when they make mistakes and fail. This infact is what life is. We fail, we learn, we rise and we grow. Sometimes, it's our attitude during difficult times that ruins their sense of self and capabilities with our words of disappointment.

Many times, our own disappointment comes from our own failures and not our children's actions.

If our children perceive judgment or a lack of acceptance, it will increase their likelihood to look for validation elsewhere.

Ordinarily, around the teenage years, they are on a default mode to seek for validation elsewhere. This is a time for us to consolidate.

As a parent, you must rid yourself of the need to prove

anything to anybody.

You must also tell the children the truth about your journey in a way that makes you connect with their struggles and validates the belief that they can overcome.

10. Setting boundaries and disciplining. Many parents become casual in a bid to create a friendship with their children. When I say 'casual', I mean in the sense of being indulgent. While other parents take a war-zone approach to it.

Rules have to be set but they do not have to be thrown at the child or teen. They should be discussed. We need to reduce the occasions we say "because, I said so". Many times we do this to tell ourselves that we are in control but the real control is in enforcing consequences when there is a default.

So yes, set rules but sit with the teens and tell them your expectations on their behavior and agree on consequences. Yes, agree on consequences. When you agree on consequences, you put some power in their hands and this can reduce the need for a power tussle which is particularly dominant in this season.

11. Enforce set standards. As teens grow older and are testing parental boundaries in view of considering themselves technically adults, you want to avoid altercations and so having dialogues and agreeing on consequences creates an illusion of choice, deliberated on and agreed upon.

In a situation of default, enforcing needs to be done without a fuss or a fight. Based on the fact that it was jointly agreed on, then it must be followed through. When followed through without a fuss or a fight, teens are most likely to be remorseful than when there was an outburst.

The outburst makes it about the parent and his or her ego and that can be entertaining for the teen and actually distract from the subject matter for which correction is directed towards.

As we agree on terms for acceptable behavior, we need to remember that consequences must be:

Respectful

Deal with the behavior and NOT/NEVER the person of the child. The conversation needs to be done in a calm and respectful way.

For example, in a situation after your child comes home past curfew time, you can actually say something like this

> "Hmmm you came in past your curfew time, what that means is no outing for another couple of days. How was your day? I hope good".

You can ask about what happened but not in the context to adjust consequences but in the context of showing love should they have been in trouble. You can also ask what happened, so that you can show them what to do another time should they be likely to miss curfew. During these times, you will both come up with possible situations that will honestly make you understand should they miss curfew but the bottom line is to come up with ways that can help them avoid missing curfew time altogether.

For instance, if they claim they were stuck in traffic then you can suggest leaving school a lot earlier otherwise consequences will still apply.

This is the direct opposite of taking it out on the person of the child. Like when parents will go something like

> "You are always late, you never take responsibility, you are not like your sibling".

I am guilty of the latter approach and I can assure you that it's the easy way out but it hardly ever builds up the teen to make the right choices.

Oh yes, I have raised at least four foster children thus far.

Taking charge as a parent means that we enforce the consequence in such a way that there is no room to say "ALWAYS". We steadily must work towards creating what is **realistic for our teen, workable for our supervision** and with **structures to enforce consequences.**

<u>Related to the misbehavior</u>

Consequences must be perceived as fair so that the children make the adjustment that they need.

If a child didn't put away his game box properly, he can be made to go a day off the game box but changing his curfew would be totally unrelated. This will make the voice for justice in his head scream over the voice of remorse, because unrelated consequences are perceived as unfair.

Reasonable

Yes, the consequence needs to be reasonable in duration and severity. Like in the previous example, one day off the game box is reasonable but one week off would be totally unfair.

Revealed in advance

Consequences also have to be revealed in advance, which is why I wrote about having dialogues earlier. When consequences are already discussed it reduces the likelihood of enforcing spontaneous unreasonable consequence which could either exaggerate or understate the impact of the behavior, both of which would make the discipline ineffective.

Repeat

Ensuring that teens clearly understand behavior expectations can make a world of difference. The dialogue allows us clarify context and goals etc. When we set the standards or rules, through dialogues we will discover different context that may or may not work well with the stated standards and as such reach an agreement on the length and breadth of the expected behavior.

Let's say you have fixed curfew for 6pm, what about

when classes are set at 5 - 6pm? What about games night, a friend's party etc. these situations do not mean that curfew will be abolished. Rather, it is opportunity to state what should happen to either meet up the curfew or state clearly adjusted curfew times on those days.

12. As parents, we must model a peer-pressure resistant culture. Our children must see that we make decisions from an informed, thought through process and not just because we were told to. We must read wide and keep an informed disposition. We must resist trying to be like anyone else. We must model the ability to be alone and yet be totally okay.

Friends don't have to be around all the time. We must model our ability to focus on what really matters so we show them that it is even possible to live wholesomely and free of influence.

Be careful of how you pick up trends be it what you add to your vocabulary or a fashion item.

As an aside, you cannot buy every asoebi for every event and then turn around to expect your children to be independent. Sometimes, ask for what the color is and look at your wardrobe and pick up the same color or something similar.

Offer to gift the people celebrating with the money you would have bought the asoebi, that will teach your children the bottom line of why you are part of celebrations other than the "feel-good" for selfie things. Better still, when you can't afford it, don't beat yourself in front of the children.

Infact, don't beat yourself at all, because when you do, many times that is the 'everyone' thing playing in your own head.

Essentially, in this chapter, I have provided the tools for creating an atmosphere that influence-proofs children. An atmosphere that shows a child that he or she is loved, accepted and they are enough.

If you are wondering what happens when a child knows they are loved but still go out and fall for the pressure, do not worry, that is what I will be focusing on in the next chapter.

- Key Points

- Be deliberate about creating an influence-proof atmosphere in your home.
- Speak deliberately and intentionally to your children.
- Communicate clearly and this involves speaking as it involves listening.
- As a parent, do not give in to peer pressure.

BUILDING RESILIENCE, FORTITUDE & IMPULSE CONTROL IN TEENS
(CHAPTER FOUR)

So far, we have talked about the ideas that become and drive influence, how influence comes, what influence looks like, what makes it thrive and what parents can do to create an enabling environment at home that allows children and teens to thrive about the voices and pulls of influence.

In this chapter, I focus on how children develop their inner strength to fight off influence especially those that happen in our absence.

Pop-culture as well as other sources of influence can be really fluid and our teens are surrounded by it. It is therefore important to build moral and emotional resilience towards news being pushed by various channels.

When your child is watching a movie for the purpose of being entertained, what lenses and boundaries must they set to protect their minds?

When friends pull and pull and they feel surrounded on all sides, what can be done to help before, during and post pressure seasons?

Here are a few suggestions:

1. <u>Create a safe net culture with the teens.</u>

A simple code that you want them to blurt when pressured, that is kind of private. In this case, family communication is top notch and you have successfully told the child "if you feel pressured, dial mom or dial dad".

2. <u>Teach or encourage your teens to create "counter-culture".</u>

Let them choose differently from their peers. Don't be fixated on them fitting in as well. If they choose a fashion sense that goes against the norm, as much as possible, don't call it weird especially if it meets the criteria listed in the previous chapter.

3. <u>Redefine authority attribution.</u>

Teach them to ask "says who" questions to ideas, beliefs and opinions that go against family values. Let them question the lyrics of music they seem to enjoy by listening for meanings. Let them question characters on the shows they watch. Encourage them to not consume blindly everything they see or hear.

On a TV show, I stumbled on recently. I heard one teen tell another that it is **easier to apologize that to take permission**. Please take note of that phrase because, I can tell you free of charge that it is going to catch on, sooner or later. It is a perfect pop-culture line.

It is an idea that will be pushed and is being pushed

already. It may sound cool to the teens, but ask your teens to troubleshoot the idea and ask 'does this really apply at all?', does it apply in every case? Why are the parents not granting permission/ what is being asked for? Is this even true? It is important for them to ask these questions.

Don't be deterred when they begin to also ask you these kinds of questions. One more reason why you yourself need to be firmly grounded on your own values and decisions.

4.   <u>Help them address their fear of being alone.</u>

Teach your children and teens good social skills and about being proactive about making friends in school. In the event that friends leave, teach them to reflect on how they contributed to this. If they wronged a friend on basis that are consistent with the right moral values then, they should apologize.

If the wrongdoing is based on their refusal to compromise on set standards, then they should take some time off and be patient while looking out to make new friends whom they share same or similar values.

5.   <u>Respect their autonomy.</u>

Do not micromanage them. Show that you trust them to manage whatever is thrown at them while assuring them you are always there to listen and they don't need to carry the burden alone.

6.   <u>Teach them to confront their assumptions.</u>

Teenagers have a problem that even adults have. In

psychology it is called Complex Equivalence. This is when people make two totally unrelated statements but assume or believe that one has to do with the other.

Typical teenage thoughts will be;

- I wish my hair was straight like hers.
- My hair is disgusting.

    OR

- I have to dress like that.
- My clothes are not as beautiful.

Our goal is to help the teenagers develop as many threads of logical possibilities as possible.

Essentially, help them develop enriching perspectives on issues. This is why encouraging reading as a family culture is an especially unique way of building children's perspectives, so that they are not narrow minded.

The more well-read children and teens are, the more they are aware that there is no singular way of looking at things and one thing could have several interpretations and perhaps more important is that they have the power to interpret something in different ways.

In addition, model to them to sleep over decisions they need to make.

7. <u>Teach them to think-it-through:</u>

Teach them to label how they feel, express and think

through what they are thinking.

When they throw up their thoughts, fears and concerns, it is important to teach them problem solving skills that allow them think through problems rather than act impulsively. That way, they can identify what the problem is, come up with several possible solutions and pick the one that most effectively solves it.

What this means is that from when they're really young, we must resist over-helping them. If they have a difficulty, help them process how to solve it. Let them develop multiple ways to solve the problem and settle for the most effective in their opinion.

8. <u>Teach them to say no</u>

How can you do this?

a) Encourage them from home to have opinions that are actually given consideration in times of decision-making. Develop their ability to think critically before making decisions.

b) Some researchers and writers recommend role-playing that enable teenagers practice saying "No". So at home, put them in a situation that you or siblings play the devil's advocate while the teen himself or herself is to maintain a stance throughout the entire activity.

You should do this with all your children and teens.

During the civil rights movements led by Martin Luther King, he had to practice the non-violent activity by putting his men in a room where people pretended to attack just as viciously as they had anticipated when they were out on the streets. During the exercise, he selected those who did not resist or try to fight back.

They had to rehearse being attacked, beaten without fighting back.

9.   <u>Practice handling public embarrassment.</u>

This one is like giving your teen the all-time life-line. This is the buffer for the ultimate blackmail of teenage years – 'the fear of embarrassment'. How about we just confront this fear head long, yes, by preparing our teens for the worst case scenario - which is being publicly embarrassed.

The first thing to learn is that the underlying purpose of being embarrassed is so that your teen 'feels' humiliated. How is humiliation measured? It is measured by how much anger, anxiety and other intense negative emotion your teen will feel in those awkward moments.

How should they handle those moments;

<u>Step One</u>

If they show no emotion in terms of anger, or anxiety or any other emotion that suggest they are upset and instead smile or laugh (not showing tension) at the people instigating the embarrassment, they deflate the unsuspecting proponents of the stunt. They must not give in to anger in those moments. It becomes fuel for the show.

Advise them not to beat themselves up publicly. Neither should they to defend themselves. Recommend they imagine something positive or something they look forward to.

Step Two

Redefine what loss of status is in the real sense of it. Many times the impact of the embarrassment hits hard because of the meaning your teen ascribes to it. Remind them that people forget easily.

Let your teen who so incredibly fears embarrassment know that sometimes, these are just empty threats and the student body can be completely unmoved by the stunts. The people who want to shame can be booed by the larger student body.

This is just one of so many possibilities that could outrightly work in their favor.

Step Three

If the embarrassment is coming from something, they did wrong, they should apologize publicly to everyone. This will be unexpected and take power out of the hands of those who want to perpetuate the humiliation. This can happen in situations where a teenager used to do wrong with peers and then he or she wants out and they try to threaten with blackmail. Such a child should be encouraged to apologise sincerely to the people involved and move on.

Step Four

For the rest of the day or term or whatever period it is,

tell your teen to avoid going over the incident in their head unless they are ready to laugh over what happened. You can cuddle them up and laugh it over with them too.

That way, they let go of the power it has over them.

<u>Step Five</u>

Encourage your teen to let go of the need to pay back. Let them forgive and let go. Whether your teen is breaking out of pressure or has always been one to live above pressure, encourage them to show empathy for the overwhelm that peer influence can cause other teens especially those who spite others. Help your teen see what an incredible gift it is to break out of the negative influence of others.

Now you do not have any reason to be afraid of the quality of decisions that your child or teen will make in your absence. You have the tools, go ahead and use them.

What if your child or teen is already drowning in this influence and you cannot seem to wrap your head around what to do to help them? This is right where our conversation is going next. You would find answers in the next chapter.

- **Key Points**

- Allow your children create counter culture.
- Encourage questioning. Allow them ask questions.
- Teach them how to prepare for confrontation. Use role playing.
- Let them be prepared to lose friends and make new ones.

OTHER UNIQUE SITUATIONS
(CHAPTER FIVE)

As much as this book is really about preparing against peer-pressure and resisting peer-pressure, it is still important to know what to also do when the teens are already swallowed by peer pressure. It is possible for them to pull back. It is possible for them to make the changes. You have to help them in a healthy way.

Here are somethings you can do to help:

Show love.

The first thing I would love to state here is that as parents we should be ready to show love and empathy. This period is usually characterised by misjudgment which means getting angry at your teen can be misunderstood by your teen and lead to a string of poor choices. You have to show love, empathy and at the same time be firm. While this doesn't mean that you should indulge, it does means that you shouldn't nag. It does mean that you should not begin attacking their friends. It does mean that you shouldn't resort to public shaming unless there is no way around it.

It does mean that you should be the subtle voice of reason.

A few years ago, I read about this father that made his son promise that he would never drive when drunk. To seal this, he instructed his teenage son to give him a call to drive him anytime he and his friends were drunk.

Ridiculous right?

So, one night, at about 2am, his son was in this club about forty-five minutes away from home and suddenly realized how drunk he was. His friends asked him to drive them home and he refused. He however, told them that he would call his dad who would drive them all home.

He then called his father and this angel of a dad drove all the way, picked them up and dropped them off without saying a word. No judgment, no fighting, no criticism and no conversation either. He had already prepared himself for this day.

The boys were sober.

In this story as told by the son, the young man said that was his last time of drinking with friends. Can you beat that?

Allow legal consequences pan out

Recently, I stumbled on a video on a project going on in the United States dubbed 'Consider the Consequences'. This program is considered controversial. Most of the people, who argue for or against it, do so passionately.

The program takes in children who have become out of control from their parents and puts them in a simulation of the justice system. So, they appear in court, take mugshots and spend some hours in the prison with real prisoners. "It's scary" they cry but the program is meant to show them the consequences of their current choices. It's supposed to show them where they could end up.

I think programs like this can interrupt the overwhelming influence that results in terrible habits. Some people say that people outgrow this influence but I don't believe the outgrowing can happen on its own.

For those who outgrow, there is usually an experience that creates an epiphany which brings them to the realization of what they are actually doing to themselves and their loved ones. That is usually when turning point decisions are made.

For some children a day in that prison can reshape their lives totally. Is it possible that it can harden them? Perhaps so. Which is why, at KNOSK, we recommend a post-parenting module for parents whose children have gone through the Consider the Consequence program if that doesn't already exist.

What is the point I am trying to make?

If your child gets into trouble, please do not try to manipulate the process. Be present but let them go through the consequences of their own actions.

If they are on suspension from school don't try to reduce the terms. Rather, have them use that time to reflect. Do not indulge them. Do not fight. Do not be indifferent as well.

A client recently talked to me about one of her children who was undergoing suspension from school. When I asked where the child was, she said he was home. And so, I thought to myself with the TV, game box and all what not. Quite frankly, that sounded to me like a vacation instead of a consequence for misbehavior.

He should go with you to work, or to a library. He shouldn't be going through a smooth sailing routine during these times. The experience should be such that he prefers going to school and as such, he won't be walking in the direction of a suspension. When a child is serving a punishment, that is not the time to win their love and loyalty. It can be counter-productive to attempt that.

Some time ago, I read about this mom and her teenage son who always had the school bus waiting and it was becoming embarrassing. She was getting feedback from the school authority about how his failure to be on time was affecting his siblings and other families who were all ready and waiting to catch the bus.

One morning, it happened again. The mom asked the bus to leave with his siblings. He must have thought that, mum was going to drive him to school but that day his mom had a different idea entirely.

Shortly after he came downstairs and saw the bus had gone off without him, his mum mentioned to him that people who refuse to go to school will clean the entire house. He thought it was a joke. She had the house keepers take a break. The young man cleaned the entire house and cars and the outdoors and was still working at the time his siblings were back from school. Needless to say, he never came out late again to catch the bus.

Please always, ensure the conditions at home do not undermine the effects of the consequences.

Dealing with foster children you didn't raise from birth can be very tricky.

Many of them come from homes who have different beliefs and values so when mixed with what the 21st century work life and time availability looks like, this can be a very difficult place to be.

Foster, in the context of this book and all of my writings, are children/teens who come to live with us. They may come as relatives, family friends and under whatever guise but they are teens you didn't give birth and came after have already reached a certain age especially pre-teen or teen years, and you are now expected to raise them. Yes, it can be difficult.

You must settle in your mind that they came for you to nurture and build up.

Avoid starting the correction from their actions, start from their thought process. This is the most strategic place to begin shaping their lives. Trust me when I say, it's going to be a long journey. Going back in time, I wish I had set ground rules first, so that we don't start out grinding and mending. Set ground rules on spoken words, TV choices, hygiene, what can be done with spare time based on the value and beliefs you are trying to pass on to them. Yes, create room for spare time. Insist on the standards every time but also ensure to create an atmosphere where they can talk to you too. Yes, talk to you freely.

Please make the time to have talks, chat with them, learn about them, learn what they think of different things, ask for their thoughts on issues, and design an affirmation for them.

When your child is the peer to be avoided.

In a situation where your child is responsible for propagating negative influence on their peers, where they are the bad examples, where they are the bullies etc.. You must take responsibility and do something about it.

I recommend:

Sit back and talk

Children and teens that are like this, have mopped up the wrong values. It is either they are mirroring something happening around them or are hurting badly.

Children who are bullied at home, may look for the nearest opportunity to vent through bullying others. This also applies to children and teens that are made fun of at home.

In a recent survey, applied to groups of teens, teens who did drugs most likely had an adult in their immediate homes or within their compound (neighbors) doing same. So, they take this vibe and try to recruit friends in the neighborhood and at school to join the tribe.

Dear parent, look around you.

Speak with your child and look for ways to create a family atmosphere that is supportive and empowering.

New behavior standards should be put in place and enforced.

If a child has unlimited access to TV, Internet and is overly exposed to his or her subject of influence, then there is need for that to be regulated. If we establish an understanding with the teen and then implement the changes while cheering them for their little victories, then we will achieve results.

Reward

Create a system that rewards them for every milestone they achieve. Reward them in ways that satisfy them. Choose what they love and use those as rewards.

Seek professional help

Look for professionals working in the field that your child is struggling in. They can help your child resolve the inner dialogues and patterns that cause the misbehavior.

Through professional help with a coach or therapist, your child should be able to redefine what they believe and think about certain things.

You cannot do this alone.

In all of this, avoid labelling your child.

Protect other children from your children.

As hurtful as this sounds, it is the responsible thing to do. Don't allow other children unsupervised access to your child.

Distract and engage them

Beneath every broken child is a dream, a talent, a skill an interest etc. Speak with your child about starting out doing something they really love. It could be in the form of volunteering, building skill or starting off a project. Howbeit, this should ride on professional help.

- Key Points

- Show love in a healthy way.
- Seek professional help.
- By all means, do not label your child rather use affirmations.
- Review your home to identify possible sources of negative influences and address them promptly.

HOW TO RECOGNIZE AND MAXIMIZE POSITIVE PEER INFLUENCE
(CHAPTER SIX)

All influences are not wrong. I mentioned that at the beginning of the book. It is therefore important for us to clearly define what positive peer pressure otherwise called 'peer energy' is like.

Often times, teens often feel like we are always telling them what not to do and we hardly ever tell them what to do.

This chapter is written for you to use in defining and teaching your children and teens how to define and nurture friendships that make for the right kind of influence.

First off, positive peer pressure is an influence that helps a person stay true to their values, pushes them to grow also allows them room for personal initiative.

There are three distinct features of positive peer pressure.

1.   Helps a teen stay true to the values they have been taught from home.

This means that friends like this will show respect to

parents and families ideal. I have personally had friends like this even as a teenager.

2.   Encourages your teen to grow

Your teens can have friends who encourage them to overcome areas of weakness in healthy ways that do not go against your personal values from home.

They can work with your teen to overcome shyness or motivate them take up an activity at school.

3.   Positive influence allows them to have a voice.

This means the influence is not manipulative and is not forceful. It comes through a dialogue. Your teen is allowed to think holistically on the recommendations. They are not harassed into it.

Some people are domineering by nature, but even in a positive peer energy environment, they should not 'make' your child do anything.

In positive peer pressure there is no form of threat or control. There is an offer of support, dialogue and accountability.

Typical examples of positive peer pressure:

1.   When friends encourage your teen to volunteer on a project so that they get to share their knowledge and skills.
2.   When friends encourage your teen to take on a holiday job.

3. When friends remind or influence your teen about treating others with respect or turning in their school work early.
4. When friends encourage your teen to join a club to improve an area they are struggling with.

While at this, prepare your child as well to be a positive influence on others.

Start by doing the things you have read in this book.

Teach your child how to spot people's values.

Teach your child how to go out of their way to connect with people they share same of similar values. And when they connect with these friends, they too must do three things;

a. Help their friends stay true to their own family's values.
b. Encourage their friends to grow.
c. They must not dominate their friends n anyway or show disrespect for their views.

In doing this, we are preparing our children to be friends of positive influence while also ensuring that they too only open up to the right kind of influence.

- Key Points

Positive influence has three distinct features;

- Helps a teen stay true to the values they have been taught from home.

- Encourages your teen to grow.

- Positive influence allows them to have a voice. It is not manipulative or forceful.

CONCLUSION

In conclusion, influences are everywhere but children who have a strong sense of love and acceptance at home are better equipped to keep their head above the sweeping current of teenage peer pressure.

As parents, we must leave the door of communication open at all times, expose our children to perspective enriching experiences and support them to keep the switch board of moral reasoning permanently turned on in their minds.

Not every teen gets carried away. Lose the fear and use the knowledge we have shared in here and guide your child through this crucial time of their life.

A teen who successfully journeys through teen years, overcoming teenage years and its shenanigans, is a stable adult who would make a super leader in every sphere of endeavor.

Keep me posted on how this goes.

Train up a child in the way he should go,
[a]And when he is old he will not depart from it.

Proverbs 22:6 | New King James Version (NKJV)

Point your children in the right direction—
when they're old they won't be lost.

Proverbs 22:6 | The Message (MSG)

ABOUT THE AUTHOR

Irene Bangwell is the Co-founder of KNOSK, an education innovation company that focuses on actionizing learning, education research and providing parenting education.

She writes, creates new tools, and designs programs that make learning spaces more empowering for children and teens. She is the designer of the Education Innovation Map, amongst other education management tools.

She has authored other parenting books including; **12 Things Every Parent Should Know, Moving from Overwhelmed to Overwhelm, Back2School Success Kit** and **Raising Girls and the Boys who would love them**.

She has worked as an on-air parenting coach since 2010 and has mentored and continues to mentor hundreds of teens since 2008. Irene Bangwell is married to Kingsley Bangwell and together they have two amazing daughters, Briona and Elena who love God, arts and want to solve global problems.

To learn more about KNOSK;
Visit: www.knoskeducation.com
Email: ask@knosk.com.ng
Phone: +234 9033338510.

www.ingramcontent.com/pod-product-compliance
Lightning Source LLC
Chambersburg PA
CBHW061438160726
47995CB00003B/949